GETTING

Safe
Pressure
Cooker
Recipes

GETTING IT RIGHT

Safe Pressure Cooker Recipes

Annette Yates

foulsham

LONDON • NEW YORK • TORONTO • SYDNEY

foulsham
Yeovil Road, Slough, Berkshire, SL1 4JH

These Recipes represent a small selection from:
Tower Pressure Cookbook

Additional recipes by Hilary Walden

Photography by Mike O'Neil

Home Economist Janet Warren

ISBN 0-572-01920-3

Printed in Great Britain at St. Edmundsbury Press, Bury St. Edmunds.

CONTENTS

WHY PRESSURE COOKING

Under-valued and misunderstood, pressure cooking still conjures up images of steamed puddings and limp vegetables. The reality is a lot different — the pressure cooker has the potential to produce the most amazing and exciting meals. This book will lift the lid off pressure cooking and show you how to cook delicious meals suitable for small families or big gatherings; fancy social events or basic economy meals.

Pressure cooking has many advantages over traditional cooking — first there's speed of cooking: the time required for cooking under pressure is roughly one third that of conventional cooking. And, of course, it is an exceptionally healthy method of preparing food: because a pressure cooker is designed to harness steam, when food is cooked on the trivet vitamins and minerals that would normally be boiled away are retained in the food. Shorter cooking times mean food is less likely to lose colour and also has less time to lose flavour.

The shorter cooking times and the ability to cook several types of food together make the pressure cooker a very economical kitchen appliance.

The recipes in this book have been selected from around the world and have been chosen to show just how versatile your pressure cooker really is. Don't be put off by the myths surrounding this style of cooking, once you start with the simple recipes, you'll want to experiment with the more unusual combinations. A complete meal can be prepared in a pressure cooker — meat or fish, vegetables and rice for example, or you can prepare just one delicate and exotic dessert.

ALL ABOUT PRESSURE COOKERS

A pressure cooker works by trapping the steam inside the main body of the appliance. An airtight seal prevents the steam escaping and pressure builds up inside. When water is heated under pressure its temperature can rise above 100°C and so food will be cooked more quickly.

Generally, pressure cookers operate at three pressures – 5 lb low pressure for cooking desserts and delicate foods, 10 lb medium pressure best for jams and jellies and 15 lb high pressure suitable for most foods, such as pulses, vegetables, soups and meats.

There are a number of types of pressure cooker on the market, all of which work on the same principle. The first has a pressure weight with an indicator plunger which rises and falls as pressure changes. Rings on the indicator show when a particular pressure has been reached and at this stage the heat must be reduced to maintain the pressure-level. Cooking time begins once the pressure is achieved. Some weights have an audible signal indicating when pressure has been reached. A different type has individual weights for different pressures which need to be fitted firmly at the beginning of cooking.

The pressure can be released in two ways, either by turning off the heat and allowing the pressure to subside slowly or by plunging into cold water to reduce pressure quickly. Slow pressure release is best used for liquid foods like stews and soups which are liable to spurt out of the vent pipe on sudden reduction of pressure. The slow method should also be used for milk puddings which are likely to curdle and for any puddings containing a raising agent.

The most modern models on the market have a unique variable pressure release system allowing the pressure to be released under control without plunging in water.

Most pressure cookers are made of aluminium which is both lightweight and strong. It is ideal for cooking as it spreads heat quickly and evenly over the base area.

Your pressure cooker will come complete with a trivet, which can be removed for soups and stocks, and perforated and unperforated baskets so that different foods can be cooked together.

Remember that to maintain the necessary pressure, a pressure cooker must contain a minimum amount of liquid to produce steam. The longer the cooking time the greater the amount of liquid needed. Amounts of liquid necessary vary from recipe to recipe; as a rule, for cooking times up to 30 minutes use a minimum of $\frac{1}{2}$ pt/300 ml/$1\frac{1}{4}$ cups liquid. Any liquid is appropriate – water can be substituted with beer, stock, cider or wine, but do not use oil as it does not produce steam when heated. (See also pages 87-92).

Rotating valve

Lid with Clamp

Sealing Gasket

SOUPS
AND STARTERS

Your pressure cooker will save you hours of time and effort as versatile soups can be made very quickly. Begin a meal with Vichyssoise, Minestrone or Oxtail Soup.

Delicious starters such as Hummous and paté can also be prepared with ease.

OXTAIL SOUP

INGREDIENTS	IMPERIAL	METRIC	AMERICAN
Cooking oil	1 tbsp	1 tbsp	1 tbsp
Oxtail, jointed	1	1	1
Onions, chopped	2	2	2
Celery sticks, sliced	2	2	2
Carrot, sliced	1	1	1
Beef stock	2 pt	1.1 l	5 cups
Bouquet garni	1	1	1
Salt and pepper			
Butter	1 oz	25 g	2 tbsp
Flour	2–3 tbsp	2–3 tbsp	2–3 tbsp
Lemon juice	1 tsp	1 tsp	1 tsp

Heat the oil in the open pressure cooker and sauté the oxtail and the vegetables gently for 4–5 minutes. Add the stock and bouquet garni and season well. Bring to pressure and cook for given time. Reduce pressure. Strain the soup. Remove the meat from the bones and cut it into small pieces.

Cool the stock (preferably overnight), then skim off the surface fat. In the open pressure cooker or a saucepan, melt the butter. Add the flour and cook gently for a few minutes, stirring well. Slowly add the oxtail stock and bring to the boil, stirring continuously. Add the meat pieces. Adjust seasoning if necessary and add lemon juice just before serving.

COOKING TIME High/15-lb pressure 40 minutes
Reduce pressure slowly

SERVES 4–6

COCK-A-LEEKIE

INGREDIENTS	IMPERIAL	METRIC	AMERICAN
Chicken joints	3	3	3
Leeks, chopped	1 lb	450 g	1 lb
Chicken stock	$1\frac{1}{2}$ pt	900 ml	$3\frac{3}{4}$ cups
Salt			
Black pepper			

Place the chicken joints and leeks in the pressure cooker and pour in the stock. Season well. Bring to pressure and cook for given time. Reduce pressure.

Remove the chicken joints from the pressure cooker and, when cooled sufficiently, remove the meat from the bones, breaking it into pieces. Return the chicken pieces to the pressure cooker. Adjust seasoning, if necessary, reheat and serve.

COOKING TIME High/15-lb pressure 7 minutes
Reduce pressure slowly

SERVES 4–6

VICHYSSOISE

INGREDIENTS	IMPERIAL	METRIC	AMERICAN
Butter	3 oz	75 g	6 tbsp
Leeks, sliced	6	6	6
Onions, sliced	2	2	2
Potatoes, thinly sliced	2	2	2
Salt and pepper			
Chicken stock	$1\frac{3}{4}$ pt	1 l	$4\frac{1}{4}$ cups
Sprigs of parsley	2–3	2–3	2–3
Single/thin cream	$\frac{1}{2}$ pt	300 ml	$1\frac{1}{4}$ cups
Chopped chives, to garnish			

Heat the butter in the open pressure cooker and sauté the vegetables for 2–3 minutes without browning them. Season and add the chicken stock and parsley sprigs. Bring to pressure and cook for given time. Reduce pressure.

Remove the parsley sprigs. Purée or sieve the soup and cool. Stir the cream into the chilled soup just before serving, garnished with chopped chives.

COOKING TIME High/15-lb pressure 6 minutes
Reduce pressure slowly

NOTE This soup may also be served hot with the cream stirred in just before serving.

SERVES 6

MINESTRONE

Ingredients	Imperial	Metric	American
Butter	1 oz	25 g	2 tbsp
Streaky bacon slices, chopped	3	3	3
Onion, chopped	1	1	1
Clove garlic, crushed	1	1	1
Leek, sliced	1	1	1
Carrot	1	1	1
Celery stick, sliced	1	1	1
Cabbage, shredded	$\frac{1}{4}$	$\frac{1}{4}$	$\frac{1}{4}$
Runner beans or green beans, sliced	4	4	4
Peas, shelled	1 oz	25 g	$\frac{1}{4}$ cup
Tomato purée/paste	2 tbsp	2 tbsp	2 tbsp
Salt and pepper			
Chicken stock or water	2 pt	1.1 l	5 cups
Macaroni, spaghetti or pasta shapes	1 oz	25 g	$\frac{1}{4}$ cup

Heat the butter in the open pressure cooker and sauté the bacon and vegetables gently for 2–3 minutes. Add the remaining ingredients, bring to pressure and cook for given time. Reduce pressure. Adjust seasoning if necessary.

COOKING TIME High/15-lb pressure 8 minutes
Reduce pressure slowly

SERVES 4–6

DHAL SOUP WITH SPICY YOGURT

INGREDIENTS	IMPERIAL	METRIC	AMERICAN
Ghee or oil	2 tbsp	2 tbsp	2 tbsp
Small onion, diced	1	1	1
Cloves garlic, finely chopped	2	2	2
Piece fresh root ginger, peeled and finely chopped	1 inch	2.5 cm	1 inch
Bay leaf	1	1	1
Cumin seeds, finely crushed	$\frac{1}{2}$–1 tsp	$\frac{1}{2}$–1 tsp	$\frac{1}{2}$–1 tsp
Cloves, bruised	2	2	2
Yellow split peas	8 oz	225 g	$\frac{1}{2}$ lb
Celery sticks	2	2	2
Leek, chopped	1	1	1
Carrot, diced	1	1	1
Vegetable stock	2 pt	1.1 l	5 cups
Grated rind and juice of 1 lemon			
Salt and pepper			
Chopped coriander leaves, to garnish			
Spiced Yogurt: Plain yogurt	4 fl oz	100 ml	$\frac{1}{2}$ cup

14

Paprika pepper	$\frac{1}{2}$ tsp	$\frac{1}{2}$ tsp	$\frac{1}{2}$ tsp
Ground turmeric	$\frac{1}{2}$ tsp	$\frac{1}{2}$ tsp	$\frac{1}{2}$ tsp
Ground cumin	$\frac{1}{4}$ tsp	$\frac{1}{4}$ tsp	$\frac{1}{4}$ tsp
Cayenne	$\frac{1}{4}$ tsp	$\frac{1}{4}$ tsp	$\frac{1}{4}$ tsp
Salt			

Heat the ghee or oil in the open pressure cooker and cook the onion, garlic, ginger, bay leaf, cumin and cloves over a moderately low heat, stirring occasionally, for 3–4 minutes. Stir in the split peas, celery, leek and carrot, cook for 1–2 minutes then stir in the stock. Bring to the boil, skim the scum from the surface, adjust the heat so the contents just boil but do not rise. Bring to pressure over the same heat and cook for given time.

For the spiced yogurt, whisk the yogurt until smooth then stir in the remaining ingredients.

Reduce pressure. Remove and discard the bay leaf. Purée the soup, return to the cooker and add the lemon rind and juice and seasoning to taste; adjust the flavourings and consistency, if necessary. Heat through gently. Serve in warmed bowls topped with a spoonful of the spiced yogurt and a sprinkling of coriander leaves.

COOKING TIME High/15-lb pressure 5 minutes
Reduce pressure slowly

SERVES 4–6

HUMMOUS

INGREDIENTS	IMPERIAL	METRIC	AMERICAN
Chick peas	4 oz	100 g	generous $\frac{1}{2}$ cup
Tahina or tahini	3 tbsp	3 tbsp	3 tbsp
Cloves garlic, chopped	2	2	2
Juice of 1 lemon			
Olive oil	2 tbsp	2 tbsp	2 tbsp
Salt and pepper			
Olive oil, paprika pepper, finely chopped fresh mint or parsley and pitta bread, to serve			

Pour boiling water over the chick peas and leave to soak for 1 hour. Drain the chick peas and place in the pressure cooker with 1 pt/550 ml/2 $\frac{1}{2}$ cups water. Bring to the boil in the open pressure cooker, remove the scum from the surface, adjust the heat so the contents just boil but do not rise in the cooker. Bring to pressure over the same heat and cook for given time. Reduce pressure.

Drain the chick peas, reserving 4 fl oz/100 ml/$\frac{1}{2}$ cup of the cooking liquor. Purée the chick peas, reserved cooking liquor, tahina, garlic, lemon juice and olive oil. Season to taste and spoon into a bowl. Trickle a circle of oil over the surface and sprinkle paprika pepper and chopped mint or parsley. Serve with pitta bread.

COOKING TIME High/15-lb pressure 20 minutes
Reduce pressure slowly

SERVES 4–6

PORK AND BACON PÂTÉ

INGREDIENTS	IMPERIAL	METRIC	AMERICAN
Streaky bacon	8 oz	225 g	$\frac{1}{2}$ lb
Pork, minced/ground	1 lb	450 g	1 lb
Small onion, minced/ground	1	1	1
Fresh white breadcrumbs	6 oz	175 g	3 cups
Mushrooms, finely chopped	2 oz	50 g	$\frac{1}{2}$ cup
Salt	2 tsp	2 tsp	2 tsp
Black pepper	1 tsp	1 tsp	1 tsp
Ground mace	2 tsp	2 tsp	2 tsp
Eggs, beaten	2	2	2

Remove the rind from the bacon and stretch the bacon with the blade of a knife. Use it to line a suitable ovenproof container (about 6 inches/15 cm diameter). Mix together the remaining ingredients and press them firmly into the prepared container, folding the ends of the bacon on to the pâté. Cover securely with foil. Pour 1 pt/550 ml/2$\frac{1}{2}$ cups water into the pressure cooker and position the trivet. Stand the pâté on top. Bring to pressure and cook for given time. Reduce pressure.

Put a plate on top of the pâté and weight it down. Cool like this before turning out. Serve with toast.

COOKING TIME High/15-lb pressure 25 minutes
Reduce pressure slowly

SERVES 8–10

BUTTER BEAN PÂTÉ

INGREDIENTS	IMPERIAL	METRIC	AMERICAN
Dried butter/lima beans	8 oz	225 g	$\frac{1}{2}$ lb
Ground cumin	2 tsp	2 tsp	2 tsp
Olive oil	3 tbsp	3 tbsp	3 tbsp
Juice of 2 lemons			
Cloves garlic, crushed	2	2	2
Chopped fresh coriander	2 tbsp	2 tbsp	2 tbsp
Salt and pepper			
Coriander sprigs and black olives, to garnish			

Pour boiling water over the beans and leave to soak for 1 hour. Drain. Place the beans in the pressure cooker with 1 pt/550 ml/2$\frac{1}{2}$ cups water. Bring to pressure and cook for given time. Reduce pressure.

Drain the beans and purée with the cumin, oil, lemon juice, garlic and coriander. Season to taste. Transfer to a bowl, cover and chill. Garnish with fresh coriander and olives. Serve with hot pitta bread, or warm Granary or wholemeal bread.

COOKING TIME High/15-lb pressure 12 minutes
Reduce pressure slowly

SERVES 4

FISH

There are several advantages of cooking fish in your pressure cooker. Fish is quickly cooked by most methods, but you will appreciate the full flavour of pressure-cooked fish. Hardly any flavour is lost if the minimum amount of liquid is used, and the fish is cooked in the steam. Make sure you retain the flavour and nutritive value by using the cooking liquor to make a delicious accompanying sauce.

Fish keeps its shape very well in the pressure cooker and fishy odours are reduced to a minimum.

SALMON WITH FENNEL

INGREDIENTS	IMPERIAL	METRIC	AMERICAN
Vegetable stock	$\frac{1}{2}$ pt	300 ml	$1\frac{1}{4}$ cups
White pepper			
Salmon steaks	4	4	4
Trimmed fennel bulbs, quartered, feathery tops reserved	10 oz	275 g	10 oz
Fromage blanc	$1\frac{1}{2}$ oz	40 g	3 tbsp
Salt			
Lemon juice			
Anise-flavoured liquor eg Ricard (optional)			

Oil the trivet and place in the pressure cooker. Pour the stock into the cooker. Sprinkle freshly ground white pepper over the salmon then place on the trivet. Put the fennel into the basket and place over the salmon. Bring to pressure and cook for given time. Reduce pressure.

Lift out the basket. Transfer the salmon to a warmed serving dish and keep warm. Boil the cooking liquor hard until reduced to about 4 tbsp. Purée the fennel with the reduced stock and fromage blanc. Heat through gently in a small saucepan, stirring, but do not allow to boil. Season with salt and white pepper and add a little lemon juice and anise liquor, if necessary. Pour the sauce around the salmon and garnish with the reserved feathery fennel tops.

COOKING TIME High/15-lb pressure 3 minutes
Reduce pressure quickly

SERVES 4

SOLE FILLETS WITH MUSHROOMS

INGREDIENTS	IMPERIAL	METRIC	AMERICAN
Olive oil			
Sole fillets, skinned	8	8	8
Lemon juice			
Black pepper			
Cottage cheese, drained and sieved	6 oz	175 g	$\frac{3}{4}$ cup
Finely grated rind of 1 lemon			—
Salt			
Dash Tabasco sauce			
Peeled prawns/shrimp, roughly chopped	$1\frac{1}{2}$ oz	40 g	$\frac{1}{4}$ cup
Medium dry white wine	$\frac{1}{4}$ pt	150 ml	$\frac{2}{3}$ cup
Button mushrooms, chopped	8 oz	225 g	2 cups
Chopped fresh tarragon or $\frac{1}{2}$ tsp dried	1 tsp	1 tsp	1 tsp
Fromage blanc	$1\frac{1}{2}$ oz	40 g	3 tbsp
Sprigs of tarragon and cooked prawns/shrimp, to garnish			

Brush the trivet with oil. Sprinkle both sides of each sole fillet with a little lemon juice and pepper. Lay half of the fillets flat on the trivet, with the skinned side facing uppermost. Mash the cottage cheese with the lemon rind, a little salt and a dash of Tabasco to taste, then stir in the prawns. Divide half of the cheese mixture between the fillets on the trivet, roll them up and secure with cocktail sticks/toothpicks. Repeat with the remaining fillets.

Pour $\frac{1}{4}$ pt/150 ml/$\frac{2}{3}$ cup water and the wine into the pressure cooker and put the trivet in place. Put the mushrooms in the basket and place over the fish. Bring to pressure and cook for given time. Reduce pressure.

Transfer the fish to a warmed serving dish, discard the cocktail sticks and keep the fish warm. Boil the cooking liquor hard in the open cooker until reduced to 3 tbsp. Purée the mushrooms coarsely with the tarragon, reduced cooking liquor and fromage blanc, to give a rough texture. Heat through gently in a small saucepan, stirring, without allowing to boil. Adjust the seasoning and add a little lemon juice, if necessary, to lift the flavour. Serve with the fish. Garnish with sprigs of tarragon and cooked prawns.

COOKING TIME High/15-lb pressure $2\frac{1}{2}$ minutes
Reduce pressure quickly

SERVES **4**

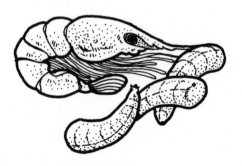

PLAKI

INGREDIENTS	IMPERIAL	METRIC	AMERICAN
Olive oil	3 tbsp	3 tbsp	3 tbsp
Onions, sliced	2	2	2
Cloves garlic, crushed	2	2	2
Carrot, sliced	1	1	1
Celery stick, sliced	1	1	1
Red pepper, de-seeded and sliced	1	1	1
Tomatoes, skinned, de-seeded, chopped	1 lb	450 g	1 lb
Tomato purée/paste	2 tsp	2 tsp	2 tsp
Chopped fresh oregano	1–2 tsp	1–2 tsp	1–2 tsp
Halibut, cut into steaks	$1\frac{1}{2}$ lb	700 g	$1\frac{1}{2}$ lb
Medium-bodied dry white wine	$\frac{1}{4}$ pt	150 ml	$\frac{2}{3}$ cup
Fish stock	$\frac{1}{4}$ pt	150 ml	$\frac{2}{3}$ cup
Salt and pepper			
Stoned/pitted black olives and chopped fresh parsley, to garnish			

Heat the oil in the open pressure cooker and sauté the onion, stirring occasionally, until beginning to colour. Add the garlic, carrot, celery and red pepper and cook over a low heat for 2–3 minutes. Add the tomatoes, tomato purée and oregano, place the fish on the vegetables and pour the wine and stock over. Bring to pressure and cook for given time. Reduce pressure.

Transfer the fish to a warmed serving dish and keep warm. Boil the cooking liquid to thicken slightly. Adjust the seasoning and amount of tomato purée and oregano, if necessary, then pour over the fish. Scatter olives and plenty of parsley over.

COOKING TIME High/15-lb pressure $2\frac{1}{2}$ minutes
Reduce pressure quickly

SERVES 4

APPLE SOLE

INGREDIENTS	IMPERIAL	METRIC	AMERICAN
Fillets sole	6	6	6
Salt and pepper			
Apple juice	$\frac{1}{2}$ pt	300 ml	$1\frac{1}{4}$ cups
Cornflour/cornstarch	2 tsp	2 tsp	2 tsp
Single/thin cream	$\frac{1}{4}$ pt	150 ml	$\frac{2}{3}$ cup
Chopped fresh parsley			

Season the sole fillets and roll them up, skin side inside. Arrange the rolls in the pressure cooker without the trivet and pour the apple juice around them. Bring to pressure and cook for given time. Reduce pressure.

Lift the fish rolls on to a warmed serving dish. Mix the cornflour with a little cold water to form a smooth paste and add it to the apple juice. Bring to the boil, stirring well. Stir in the cream, reheat the sauce gently and pour it over the fish. Sprinkle with a little chopped parsley and serve.

COOKING TIME High/15-lb pressure 4 minutes
Reduce pressure quickly

CHECKPOINT Do not boil the sauce when reheating or the cream will separate.

SERVES 4

PIQUANT PLAICE

INGREDIENTS	IMPERIAL	METRIC	AMERICAN
Plaice fillets	$1\frac{1}{2}$ lb	700 g	$1\frac{1}{2}$ lb
Salt and pepper			
Butter	1 oz	25 g	2 tbsp
Small onion, chopped	1	1	1
Clove garlic, crushed	1	1	1
Tomato purée/paste	2 tbsp	2 tbsp	2 tbsp
Worcestershire sauce	2 tsp	2 tsp	2 tsp
Sugar	$\frac{1}{2}$ tsp	$\frac{1}{2}$ tsp	$\frac{1}{2}$ tsp
Water	$\frac{1}{2}$ pt	300 ml	$1\frac{1}{4}$ cups
Cornflour/cornstarch	1 tbsp	1 tbsp	1 tbsp
Lemon wedges, to garnish			

Skin the plaice fillets and season with salt and pepper. Roll them up and secure each with wooden cocktail sticks/toothpicks. Heat the butter in the open pressure cooker and sauté the onion and garlic gently until transparent. Add remaining ingredients, except the cornflour and lemon wedges, and stir well. Sit the plaice rolls in the sauce. Bring to pressure and cook for given time. Reduce pressure.

Arrange the plaice rolls on a warmed serving dish. Mix the cornflour with a little cold water to form a smooth paste and add it to the sauce. Bring to the boil, stirring well. Pour over and around the plaice and garnish with lemon wedges.

COOKING TIME High/15-lb pressure 4 minutes
Reduce pressure quickly

SERVES 4

HADDOCK IN CREOLE SAUCE

INGREDIENTS	IMPERIAL	METRIC	AMERICAN
Cooking oil	2 tbsp	2 tbsp	2 tbsp
Small onion, chopped	1	1	1
Clove garlic, crushed	1	1	1
Celery stick, chopped	1	1	1
Green pepper, de-seeded and chopped	1	1	1
Can tomatoes	14 oz	397 g	1 lb
Tomato purée/paste	1 tbsp	1 tbsp	1 tbsp
Sugar	1 tsp	1 tsp	1 tsp
Pinch basil			
Chilli powder	$\frac{1}{2}$ tsp	$\frac{1}{2}$ tsp	$\frac{1}{2}$ tsp
Salt and pepper			
Haddock fillets, skinned and cut into cubes	4	4	4

Heat the oil in the open pressure cooker and sauté the onion, garlic, celery and pepper gently for 2–3 minutes. Stir in the tomatoes, including the juice made up to $\frac{1}{2}$ pt/300 ml/1 $\frac{1}{4}$ cups with water. Add the tomato purée, sugar, basil, chilli powder, seasoning and haddock pieces. Bring to pressure and cook for given time. Reduce pressure.

COOKING TIME High/15-lb pressure 4 minutes
Reduce pressure quickly

SERVES 4

STUFFED MACKEREL

INGREDIENTS	IMPERIAL	METRIC	AMERICAN
Mackerel, cleaned	4	4	4
Salt and pepper			
Eating apples, grated	2	2	2
Small onion, finely chopped	1	1	1
Fresh white breadcrumbs	2 oz	50 g	1 cup
Cheddar cheese, grated	4 oz	100 g	1 cup
Butter, melted	2–3 oz	50–75 g	$\frac{1}{4}$–$\frac{1}{3}$ cup
Lemon twists and chopped fresh parsley, to garnish			

Wipe the inside of the mackerel and season it inside and out with salt and pepper. Mix together the apple, onion, breadcrumbs and grated cheese. Season to taste, then bind the mixture with 2 tbsp of the melted butter. Stuff the fish and secure it with wooden cocktail sticks/toothpicks. Place each fish on a separate sheet of foil. Pour the remaining melted butter over the mackerel. Fold the foil over and seal it to make four parcels.

Pour $\frac{1}{2}$ pt/300 ml/1$\frac{1}{4}$ cups water into the pressure cooker and position the trivet. Place the parcels on the trivet. Bring to pressure and cook for given time. Reduce pressure.

Open the parcels and arrange the mackerel on a warmed serving dish. Pour any butter left in the foil over the fish and garnish them with lemon twists and parsley.

COOKING TIME High/15-lb pressure 6 minutes
Reduce pressure quickly

SERVES 4

SOUSED HERRINGS

INGREDIENTS	IMPERIAL	METRIC	AMERICAN
Small herrings	8	8	8
Salt and pepper			
Dried red chilli	1	1	1
Blade mace	1	1	1
Bay leaf	1	1	1
Whole allspice	3	3	3
Black peppercorns	6	6	6
Small onions, thinly sliced	1–2	1–2	1–2
Malt vinegar	$\frac{1}{4}$ pt	150 ml	$\frac{2}{3}$ cup
Water	$\frac{1}{4}$ pt	150 ml	$\frac{2}{3}$ cup

Scale and clean the herrings, removing the heads and tails. Split and bone the fish. Lightly season the fillets on the fleshy side with salt and pepper. Roll each up from the tail end, skin side outside, and secure each roll with a wooden cocktail stick/toothpick. Place the herrings in the pressure cooker without the trivet and add the remaining ingredients. Bring to pressure and cook for given time. Reduce pressure.

Arrange the herrings in a serving dish and pour the liquor over the fish. Allow it to cool and serve as a starter or with a salad and boiled potatoes as a main dish.

COOKING TIME High/15-lb pressure 6 minutes
Reduce pressure quickly

NOTE Boned mackerel or pilchards may also be prepared in this way.

SERVES 4

MEAT

The pressure cooker is perfect for cooking casseroles and pot roasts — from the traditional Old Fashioned Beef Casserole to Beef Bourguignon. Many dishes can be prepared in a fraction of the normal cooking time.

Try cooking the more exotic Rogan Josh and see how the subtle flavours of Oriental cookery are enhanced by pressure cooking.

LAMB HOTPOT

INGREDIENTS	IMPERIAL	METRIC	AMERICAN
Middle neck lamb chops	8	8	8
Cooking oil	2 tbsp	2 tbsp	2 tbsp
Onions, sliced	8 oz	225 g	$\frac{1}{2}$ lb
Carrots, sliced	4 oz	100 g	$\frac{1}{4}$ lb
Potatoes, sliced	1 lb	450 g	1 lb
Salt and pepper			
Stock	$\frac{3}{4}$ pt	400 ml	2 cups

Trim excess fat off the chops. Heat the oil in the open pressure cooker and brown the chops on all sides. Add the onions, carrots and potatoes and cook gently for a further 3–4 minutes. Season well and add the stock. Bring to pressure and cook for given time. Reduce pressure.

If necessary remove some of the surface fat with kitchen paper. Arrange the chops, vegetables and stock in a serving dish, finishing with a layer of potatoes. Brown under a hot grill/broiler before serving.

COOKING TIME High/15-lb pressure 15 minutes
Reduce pressure slowly

SERVES 4

BEEF BOURGUIGNON

INGREDIENTS	IMPERIAL	METRIC	AMERICAN
Butter	2 oz	50 g	$\frac{1}{4}$ cup
Chuck steak, cubed	$1\frac{3}{4}$ lb	800 g	$1\frac{3}{4}$ lb
Onions, chopped	2	2	2
Clove garlic, crushed	1	1	1
Streaky bacon, chopped	4 oz	100 g	$\frac{1}{4}$ lb
Red wine	$\frac{3}{4}$ pt	425 ml	2 cups
Bouquet garni	1	1	1
Salt and pepper			
Button mushrooms	8 oz	225 g	2 cups
Flour	2–3 tbsp	2–3 tbsp	2–3 tbsp
Chopped fresh parsley, to garnish			

Heat the butter in the open pressure cooker and brown the meat for 3–4 minutes. Lift it out with a draining spoon. In the same butter sauté the onions, garlic and bacon gently until transparent. Return the meat to the pressure cooker and add the red wine, bouquet garni, seasoning and mushrooms. Bring to pressure and cook for given time. Reduce pressure. Remove bouquet garni.

Mix the flour with a little cold water to form a smooth paste and add to the beef. Bring to the boil, stirring well.

COOKING TIME High/15-lb pressure 20 minutes
Reduce pressure slowly

SERVES 4

STEAK AND KIDNEY PUDDING

INGREDIENTS	IMPERIAL	METRIC	AMERICAN
Filling:			
Stewing steak, cut into cubes	12 oz	350 g	$\frac{3}{4}$ lb
Sheep kidneys, skinned and chopped	4 oz	100 g	$\frac{1}{4}$ lb
Seasoned flour			
Onion, chopped	1	1	1
Salt and pepper			
Beef stock	$\frac{1}{2}$ pt	300 ml	$1\frac{1}{4}$ cups
Suet pastry:			
Self-raising flour, or plain flour sifted with 2 tsp baking powder	8 oz	225 g	2 cups
Pinch salt			
Shredded suet	4 oz	100 g	$\frac{3}{4}$–1 cup
Cold water	$\frac{1}{4}$ pt	150 ml	$\frac{2}{3}$ cup

Coat the steak and the kidney pieces with seasoned flour. Place the meat, onion, seasoning and beef stock into the open pressure cooker. Bring to pressure and cook for given time. Reduce pressure.

Meanwhile, sieve together the flour and salt and stir in the suet. Mix with the cold water to form an elastic dough. Roll two-thirds of the dough into a circle and use it to line a greased $1\frac{1}{2}$-pt/1-l/4-cup basin. Put the steak and kidney in the middle with half of the gravy. Dampen the edges of the dough. Roll remaining dough into a circle and use it to cover the pudding. Press edges together firmly and trim. Cover securely with a piece of foil (make a pleat in the foil to allow the pudding to rise). Pour in $2\frac{1}{2}$ pt/1.5 1/6$\frac{1}{4}$ cups water into the pressure cooker, position the trivet and stand the pudding on top. Close the pressure cooker (do not position the weight) and place it on the heat. When steam begins to escape from the vent in the lid, lower the heat and steam it gently (without the weight) for 15 minutes. Increase the heat, bring to pressure and cook for given time. Reduce pressure.

Serve the pudding from the basin. Heat remaining gravy and serve separately.

COOKING TIME Meat mixture: High/15-lb pressure 15 minutes
Reduce pressure slowly

Pudding: Pre-steaming 15 minutes
Low/5-lb pressure 25 minutes
Reduce pressure slowly

NOTE Pre-steaming is important since this helps give a light result to the suet pastry.

SERVES 4

33

OLD FASHIONED BEEF CASSEROLE

INGREDIENTS	IMPERIAL	METRIC	AMERICAN
Lard or dripping	1 oz	25 g	2 tbsp
Stewing steak, cut into cubes	$1\frac{1}{2}$ lb	700 g	$1\frac{1}{2}$ lb
Onions, sliced	2	2	2
Carrots, sliced	2	2	2
Leeks, sliced	2	2	2
Celery sticks, sliced	2	2	2
Small swede, sliced	$\frac{1}{2}$	$\frac{1}{2}$	$\frac{1}{2}$
Large potatoes, quartered	2	2	2
Beef stock	1 pt	550 ml	$2\frac{1}{2}$ cups
Salt and pepper			
Bouquet garni	1	1	1

Heat the lard or dripping in the open pressure cooker and brown the meat for 4–5 minutes. Lift out with a draining spoon. In the same fat sauté the vegetables gently for 3–4 minutes, then stir in the browned meat, beef stock, seasoning and bouquet garni. Bring to pressure and cook for given time. Reduce pressure. Remove bouquet garni.

COOKING TIME High/15-lb pressure 15 minutes
Reduce pressure slowly

SERVES 4–6

VEAL AND MUSHROOM CREAM

INGREDIENTS	IMPERIAL	METRIC	AMERICAN
Pie veal, cut into cubes	$1\frac{1}{2}$ lb	700 g	$1\frac{1}{2}$ lb
Seasoned flour			
Butter	2 oz	50 g	$\frac{1}{4}$ cup
Onion, chopped	1	1	1
Clove garlic, crushed (optional)	1	1	1
Pinch dried thyme			
Dry cider	$\frac{1}{2}$ pt	300 ml	$1\frac{1}{4}$ cups
Salt and pepper			
Mushrooms, sliced	8 oz	225 g	2 cups
Single/thin cream	6 fl oz	175 ml	$\frac{3}{4}$ cup
Watercress, to garnish			

Coat the veal with seasoned flour. Heat the butter in the open pressure cooker and lightly brown the veal. Add the onion and garlic and cook for a further minute. Add the thyme, cider and seasoning, then stir in the mushrooms. Bring to pressure and cook for given time. Reduce pressure. Stir in the cream just before serving. Garnish with watercress.

COOKING TIME High/15-lb pressure 12 minutes
Reduce pressure slowly

SERVES 4

LAMB CUTLETS ITALIAN STYLE

INGREDIENTS	IMPERIAL	METRIC	AMERICAN
Cooking oil	2 tbsp	2 tbsp	2 tbsp
Salt and pepper			
Lamb cutlets	8	8	8
Large onion, chopped	1	1	1
Clove garlic, crushed	1	1	1
Large carrot, chopped	1	1	1
Can tomatoes	14 oz	397 g	1 lb
Dried oregano	1 tsp	1 tsp	1 tsp
Flour	2 tbsp	2 tbsp	2 tbsp

Heat the oil in the open pressure cooker and brown the well seasoned cutlets on each side. Remove from pressure cooker. In the same oil sauté the onion, garlic and carrot for 2–3 minutes. Add the tomatoes (including juice) and oregano. Place the trivet on top of the vegetables and arrange the cutlets on the trivet. Bring to pressure and cook for given time. Reduce pressure.

Transfer the cutlets to a serving dish and keep them warm. Mix the flour with a little cold water to form a smooth paste and stir it into the sauce. Bring to the boil, stirring continuously. Pour the sauce over the cutlets and serve.

COOKING TIME High/15-lb pressure 10 minutes
Reduce pressure quickly

SERVES 4

ROGAN JOSH

INGREDIENTS	IMPERIAL	METRIC	AMERICAN
Cornflour/cornstarch	1 tsp	1 tsp	1 tsp
Plain yogurt	12 fl oz	350 ml	$1\frac{1}{2}$ cups
Ghee or oil	3 tbsp	3 tbsp	3 tbsp
Large onion, thinly sliced	1	1	1
Cloves garlic, crushed	3	3	3
Piece fresh root ginger, peeled and finely chopped	1 inch	2.5 cm	1 inch
Ground coriander	1 tbsp	1 tbsp	1 tbsp
Ground cumin	2 tsp	2 tsp	2 tsp
Ground cardamom	2 tsp	2 tsp	2 tsp
Ground chilli powder	1 tsp	1 tsp	1 tsp
Ground cloves	1 tsp	1 tsp	1 tsp
Tomato purée/paste	1 tbsp	1 tbsp	1 tbsp
Lean lamb, cut into large cubes	$1\frac{1}{4}$ lb	550 g	$1\frac{1}{4}$ lb
Ground almonds	3–4 tbsp	3–4 tbsp	3–4 tbsp
Fresh coriander leaves	2 tbsp	2 tbsp	2 tbsp

Blend the cornflour with 2 tbsp water. Stir in the yogurt then heat very gently, stirring very slowly in one direction, until just on simmering point. Simmer gently, stirring in the same way, for a few minutes. Pour from the cooker.

Heat half of the ghee or oil in the pressure cooker, add the onion and cook until lightly browned. Add the garlic, cook for 1–2 minutes then stir in the spices and tomato purée. Remove from the heat and stir in the yogurt. Place the lamb in a non-metallic dish that it just fits, pour the spiced yogurt over, turning the meat to coat evenly. Cover and leave in a cool place for 4 hours.

Remove the meat from the marinade, allowing the excess to drain off. Heat the remaining ghee or oil in the pressure cooker, add the lamb and cook, stirring, for 1–2 minutes, then stir in the marinade. Slowly bring to pressure and cook for given time. Reduce pressure.

Remove the meat and keep warm. Stir the ground almonds into the cooking juices and heat gently until thickened slightly. Lower the heat and add the coriander leaves. Stir the meat back into the sauce to coat it evenly and adjust the seasoning.

COOKING TIME High/15-lb pressure 3 minutes
Reduce pressure quickly

SERVES 4

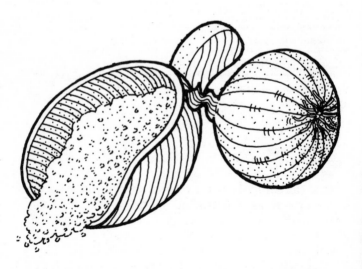

POULTRY
AND GAME

Poultry and game dishes benefit enormously from pressure cooking, retaining their full flavour and remaining tender.

Succulent game dishes such as Pheasant with Apple Cream and Pigeon Ragout are cooked in minutes.

Zaffrani Murgh, chicken with saffron, is one of the most delicious dishes you can prepare in a pressure cooker.

CHICKEN ITALIENNE

INGREDIENTS	IMPERIAL	METRIC	AMERICAN
Butter	2 oz	50 g	$\frac{1}{4}$ cup
Chicken thighs	8	8	8
Cloves garlic, crushed	2	2	2
Onions, chopped	2	2	2
Streaky bacon, chopped	4 oz	100 g	$\frac{1}{4}$ lb
Tomatoes, skinned and sliced	4	4	4
Mushrooms, sliced	4 oz	100 g	1 cup
Tomato purée/paste	4 tbsp	4 tbsp	4 tbsp
Chicken stock	$\frac{3}{4}$ pt	400 ml	2 cups
Dried oregano	1 tsp	1 tsp	1 tsp
Salt and pepper			
Flour	2 tbsp	2 tbsp	2 tbsp

Heat the butter in the open pressure cooker and brown the chicken on all sides. Remove it from the pressure cooker. In the same butter, sauté the garlic, onions and bacon gently for about 2 minutes. Stir in the tomatoes, mushrooms, tomato purée, chicken stock, oregano and seasoning. Return the chicken to pressure cooker, bring to pressure and cook for given time. Reduce pressure.

Mix the flour with a little cold water to form a smooth paste and stir it into the chicken. Bring to the boil, stirring continuously.

COOKING TIME High/15-lb pressure 7 minutes
Reduce pressure quickly

SERVES 4

CYPRUS CHICKEN

INGREDIENTS	IMPERIAL	METRIC	AMERICAN
Butter	2 oz	50 g	$\frac{1}{4}$ cup
Chicken joints	4	4	4
Medium onion, chopped	1	1	1
Mushrooms, sliced	8 oz	225 g	2 cups
Medium dry sherry	$\frac{1}{4}$ pt	150 ml	$\frac{2}{3}$ cup
Salt			
Black pepper			
Double/thick cream	$\frac{1}{2}$ pt	300 ml	$1\frac{1}{4}$ cups
Paprika	$\frac{1}{2}$–1 tsp	$\frac{1}{2}$–1 tsp	$\frac{1}{2}$–1 tsp
Chopped fresh parsley	2 tbsp	2 tbsp	2 tbsp

Heat the butter in the open pressure cooker and brown the chicken joints well on all sides. Remove. In the same butter sauté the onion gently for 2–3 minutes. Stir in the mushrooms and sherry and season with salt and pepper. Bring to pressure and cook for given time. Reduce pressure.

Lift the chicken joints on to a serving dish and keep warm. Stir the remaining ingredients into the sherry mixture. Adjust seasoning if necessary then reheat, without boiling, and pour over the chicken.

COOKING TIME High/15-lb pressure 7 minutes
Reduce pressure quickly

SERVES 4

ZAFFRANI MURGH
(Chicken with Saffron and Spices)

INGREDIENTS	IMPERIAL	METRIC	AMERICAN
Saffron threads	$\frac{1}{2}$ tsp	$\frac{1}{2}$ tsp	$\frac{1}{2}$ tsp
Piece fresh root ginger, peeled and finely chopped	2 inch	5 cm	2 inch
Cinnamon stick, broken	2 inch	5 cm	2 inch
Whole cardamom pods, lightly crushed	6	6	6
Cloves, lightly crushed	6	6	6
Ground coriander seeds	1 tbsp	1 tbsp	1 tbsp
Ground cumin seeds	1 tbsp	1 tbsp	1 tbsp
Cayenne pepper	$\frac{1}{2}$ tsp	$\frac{1}{2}$ tsp	$\frac{1}{2}$ tsp
Ghee, clarified butter or oil	2 tbsp	2 tbsp	2 tbsp
Plain yogurt	12 fl oz	350 ml	$1\frac{1}{2}$ cups
Bay leaves, torn	2	2	2
Large onion, sliced	1	1	1
Cloves garlic, crushed	2	2	2
Large chicken leg portions, skinned	4	4	4
Cornflour/cornstarch	1 tsp	1 tsp	1 tsp
Block creamed coconut, chopped	1 oz	25 g	1 oz
Salt and pepper			

*Sprigs of fresh coriander
or flat-leafed parsley,
to garnish*

In a small, heavy pan, heat the spices for about 3 minutes. Remove from the heat and stir in the ghee, yogurt, bay leaves, onion and garlic.

Place the chicken in a non-metallic dish that it just fits, pour the spiced yogurt mixture over, turning the chicken in the yogurt to coat completely. Cover the dish and leave in a cool place for about 4 hours.

Remove the chicken from the marinade, allowing excess to drain off. Blend the cornflour with 2 tbsp water then stir in the marinade. Pour into the pressure cooker, over a very low heat, stirring slowly in one direction. Bring to just on simmering point then simmer gently, still stirring slowly, for a few minutes. Turn the chicken in the yogurt to coat it. Bring to pressure and cook for given time. Reduce pressure.

Transfer the chicken to a warmed serving dish and keep warm. Over a low heat, stir the coconut into the cooking juices. Heat gently, stirring, for 2–3 minutes. Adjust the seasonings and flavourings. Divide the chicken legs into drumsticks and thighs then stir them into the cooker to coat in the sauce. Serve scattered with fresh coriander or flat-leafed parsley sprigs.

COOKING TIME High/15-lb pressure 5 minutes
Reduce pressure quickly

SERVES 4

CHICKEN AVGOLOMONO

INGREDIENTS	IMPERIAL	METRIC	AMERICAN
Juice of $\frac{1}{2}$ lemon			
Chicken breasts, skinned	4	4	4
Chicken stock	$\frac{1}{2}$ pt	300 ml	$1\frac{1}{4}$ cups
Bouquet garni	1	1	1
Egg yolks, beaten	3	3	3
Lemon juice	4 tbsp	4 tbsp	4 tbsp
Salt and white pepper			
Sprigs of parsley, to garnish			

Squeeze lemon juice over both sides of the chicken; leave for 30 minutes, if possible.

Pour the stock into the cooker and add the bouquet garni and chicken. Bring to pressure and cook for given time. Reduce pressure.

Transfer the chicken to a warmed serving plate and keep warm. Boil the cooking juices in the open cooker until reduced to 7 fl oz/200 ml/scant cup. Remove the bouquet garni. Blend the egg yolks and lemon juice together in a bowl. Whisk in a little of the reduced cooking juices then pour back into the cooker. Cook over a low heat, stirring with a wooden spoon, until thickened. Do not allow to boil. Adjust the seasoning, pour through a sieve over the chicken and garnish.

COOKING TIME High/15-lb pressure 4 minutes
Reduce pressure slowly

NOTE Make the bouquet garni with 1 bay leaf, a sprig of parsley, sprig of thyme and rosemary.

SERVES 4

TURKEY MARENGO

INGREDIENTS	IMPERIAL	METRIC	AMERICAN
Turkey joints	4	4	4
Salt and pepper			
Cooking oil	2 tbsp	2 tbsp	2 tbsp
Clove garlic, crushed	1	1	1
Large onion, sliced	1	1	1
Carrots, sliced	2	2	2
Can tomatoes	14 oz	397 g	1 lb
Chicken stock	$\frac{1}{4}$ pt	150 ml	$\frac{2}{3}$ cup
Button mushrooms	4 oz	100 g	1 cup
Bay leaf	1	1	1
Bouquet garni	1	1	1
Flour	2 tbsp	2 tbsp	2 tbsp

Season the turkey joints well with salt and pepper. Heat
the oil in the open pressure cooker and brown the turkey
joints on all sides. Remove them from the pressure
cooker. In the same oil, sauté the garlic, onion and
carrots gently for about 2 minutes. Add the browned
turkey joints, tomatoes, chicken stock, mushrooms, bay
leaf and bouquet garni. Bring to pressure and cook for
given time. Reduce pressure. Discard bay leaf and bouquet garni. Mix the flour with a little cold water to form
a smooth paste. Stir into the turkey mixture and bring to
the boil.

COOKING TIME High/15-lb pressure 10 minutes
Reduce pressure quickly

SERVES 4

PIGEON RAGOUT

INGREDIENTS	IMPERIAL	METRIC	AMERICAN
Butter	2 oz	50 g	$\frac{1}{4}$ cup
Small pigeons	4	4	4
Streaky bacon slices, chopped	4	4	4
Tomatoes, skinned and sliced	4	4	4
Beef stock	$\frac{3}{4}$ pt	400 ml	2 cups
Red wine	4 tbsp	4 tbsp	4 tbsp
Salt and pepper			
Flour	1 oz	25 g	$\frac{1}{4}$ cup

Heat the butter in the open pressure cooker and lightly brown the pigeons on all sides. Remove from pressure cooker. In the same butter, sauté the bacon gently for about 2 minutes, then stir in the tomatoes, beef stock and red wine. Return the pigeons to the pressure cooker and season with salt and pepper. Bring to pressure and cook for given time. Reduce pressure.

Using a draining spoon, lift the pigeons on to a serving dish. Mix the flour with a little cold water to form a smooth paste. Add it to the sauce and bring to the boil, stirring continuously. Adjust seasoning if necessary. Pour the sauce over and around the pigeons and serve with pieces of fried bread and watercress, if liked.

COOKING TIME High/15-lb pressure 10 minutes
Reduce pressure slowly

SERVES 4

PHEASANT WITH APPLE CREAM

INGREDIENTS	IMPERIAL	METRIC	AMERICAN
Small pheasants	2	2	2
Seasoned flour			
Butter	2 oz	50 g	$\frac{1}{4}$ cup
Cooking apples, peeled, cored and sliced	4	4	4
Beef stock	$\frac{1}{2}$ pt	300 ml	$1\frac{1}{4}$ cups
Double/thick cream	$\frac{1}{4}$ pt	150 ml	$\frac{2}{3}$ cup
Watercress, to garnish			

Coat the pheasants with seasoned flour. Heat the butter in the open pressure cooker and brown the pheasant on all sides. Lift them out. In the same butter, sauté the apples gently for 2–3 minutes. Replace the pheasants and pour the beef stock around them. Bring to pressure and cook for given time. Reduce pressure.

Place the pheasants on a serving dish and keep them warm. Purée or mash the apple mixture and adjust the seasoning if necessary. Stir in the cream. Garnish the pheasants with watercress and serve the sauce separately.

COOKING TIME High/15-lb pressure 8 minutes
Reduce pressure quickly

SERVES 4

DUCKLING CASSEROLE

INGREDIENTS	IMPERIAL	METRIC	AMERICAN
Butter	1 oz	25 g	2 tbsp
Duckling joints	4	4	4
Onions, sliced	2	2	2
Carrots, sliced	2	2	2
Chicken stock	$\frac{3}{4}$ pt	400 ml	2 cups
Bay leaf	1	1	1
Chopped fresh parsley	2 tsp	2 tsp	2 tsp
Dried oregano	$\frac{1}{2}$ tsp	$\frac{1}{2}$ tsp	$\frac{1}{2}$ tsp
Salt and pepper			
Cornflour/cornstarch	3 tbsp	3 tbsp	3 tbsp

Heat the butter in the open pressure cooker and brown the duckling joints well on all sides. Remove the duckling from the pressure cooker. In the same butter, sauté the onions and carrots gently for about 2 minutes. Add the browned duckling joints, chicken stock, bay leaf, parsley and oregano. Season well, bring to pressure and cook for given time. Reduce pressure. Discard the bay leaf.

Using kitchen paper or a metal spoon, remove excess fat from the surface of the sauce. Mix the cornflour with a little cold water to form a smooth paste. Add it to the pressure cooker and bring to the boil, stirring continuously.

COOKING TIME High/15-lb pressure 12 minutes
Reduce pressure slowly

SERVES 4

VEGETABLES

As vegetables are cooked in steam in a pressure cooker, the colour, flavour, texture and nutrients are retained. Pulses — dried peas, beans and lentils — need only 1 hour soaking in boiling water before speedy pressure cooking; unlike the lengthy process of soaking overnight required if boiling them in the usual way.

This chapter contains recipes for soups, snacks and both light and main vegetarian dishes.

QUICK VEGETABLE RAGOUT

INGREDIENTS	IMPERIAL	METRIC	AMERICAN
Celeriac	1 lb	450 g	1 lb
Acidulated water			
Carrots	1 lb	450 g	1 lb
Small turnips	1 lb	450 g	1 lb
Olive oil	3 tbsp	3 tbsp	3 tbsp
Large shallots, peeled	8	8	8
Vegetable stock	$\frac{1}{2}$ pt	300 ml	$1\frac{1}{4}$ cups
Bay leaves	2	2	2
Full fat soft cheese with herbs and garlic	150 g	5 oz	$\frac{2}{3}$ cup

Peel the celeriac, cut into large chunks and put immediately into the acidulated water. Peel the carrots and turnips and cut into similar sized chunks. Over a fairly high heat, heat the oil in the open pressure cooker and cook the vegetables, turning them over, for 1–2 minutes. Add the stock and bay leaves. Bring to pressure and cook for given time. Reduce pressure.

Transfer the vegetables to a warmed serving dish and keep warm. Remove and discard the bay leaves. Over a low heat, whisk the cheese into the stock. Pour over the vegetables.

COOKING TIME High/15-lb pressure $2\frac{1}{2}$ minutes
Reduce pressure quickly

SERVES 4

POTATO PIE

INGREDIENTS	IMPERIAL	METRIC	AMERICAN
Butter			
Potatoes, peeled and sliced thinly	$1\frac{1}{2}$ lb	700 g	$1\frac{1}{2}$ lb
Onions, chopped	2	2	2
Grated nutmeg			
Salt and pepper			
Vegetable stock	$\frac{1}{4}$ pt	150 ml	$\frac{2}{3}$ cup
Cheese, grated	2 oz	50 g	$\frac{1}{2}$ cup

Butter an ovenproof dish which will fit into the pressure cooker. Layer the potatoes and onions in the dish. Sprinkle each layer with a little grated nutmeg and season well with salt and pepper. Pour the vegetable stock over the potatoes.

Pour $\frac{1}{2}$ pt/300 ml/$1\frac{1}{4}$ cups water into pressure cooker and place the trivet in position. Stand the dish on the trivet, bring to pressure and cook for given time. Reduce pressure. Sprinkle the cheese over the potatoes and brown them under the grill/broiler before serving.

COOKING TIME High/15-lb pressure 13 minutes
Reduce pressure quickly

NOTE New potatoes might need slightly longer cooking times than those given.

This dish is also delicious made with garlic (omitting the nutmeg) and using canned tomatoes instead of the vegetable stock.

SERVES 4

VEGETABLE HOTPOT

INGREDIENTS	IMPERIAL	METRIC	AMERICAN
Dried butter/lima beans	4 oz	100 g	$\frac{1}{4}$ lb
Butter	1 oz	25 g	2 tbsp
Large onion, sliced	1	1	1
Carrots, sliced	8 oz	225 g	$\frac{1}{2}$ lb
Dried mixed herbs	$\frac{1}{2}$ tsp	$\frac{1}{2}$ tsp	$\frac{1}{2}$ tsp
Stock			
Salt and pepper			
Short macaroni	4 oz	100 g	$\frac{1}{4}$ lb
Frozen peas	4 oz	100 g	$\frac{1}{4}$ lb
Croûtes: Butter, softened	1 oz	25 g	2 tbsp
Cheddar cheese, grated	2 oz	50 g	$\frac{1}{2}$ cup
Made mustard	1 tsp	1 tsp	1 tsp
Thick slices French bread	4	4	4

Place the butter beans in a large dish and cover with plenty of boiling water. Cover with a plate and leave for 1 hour. Heat the butter in the open pressure cooker and gently sauté the onion, carrots and herbs for 3–4 minutes. Drain the butter beans and add these to the pressure cooker. Make up the soaking liquid from the beans to 1 pt/550 ml/2$\frac{1}{2}$ cups with stock. Add this to the bean mixture and season with salt and pepper. Bring to pressure and cook for given time. Reduce pressure.

Add the macaroni and peas to the vegetables, bring to

pressure again and cook for given time. Reduce pressure. Pour the vegetables into a flameproof casserole.

Beat together the softened butter, cheese and mustard and spread on to one side of the bread slices. Place the bread, butter side up, on top of the casserole. Place under a hot grill/broiler until the cheese melts. Serve more cheese separately.

COOKING TIME High/15-lb pressure 15 minutes
Reduce pressure slowly
    macaroni added 5 minutes
Reduce pressure slowly

SERVES 4

SAVOURY BROWN RICE

INGREDIENTS	IMPERIAL	METRIC	AMERICAN
Vegetable stock or water (optional)	3 pt	1.7 l	$7\frac{1}{2}$ cups
Brown rice	8 oz	225 g	generous 1 cup
Plain yogurt	4 tbsp	4 tbsp	4 tbsp
Lemon juice	1 tbsp	1 tbsp	1 tbsp
Olive oil	1 tbsp	1 tbsp	1 tbsp
Chopped fresh mixed herbs	2 tbsp	2 tbsp	2 tbsp
Wholegrain mustard	2 tbsp	2 tbsp	2 tbsp
Salt and pepper			

Button mushrooms, thinly sliced	8 oz	225 g	2 cups
Small, ripe avocado, peeled, chopped and tossed in lemon juice	1	1	1
Hazelnuts, chopped	4 oz	100 g	1 cup
Cooked peas or thawed frozen peas	2 oz	50 g	$\frac{1}{2}$ cup
Dried apricots, chopped	2 oz	50 g	$\frac{1}{3}$ cup
Watercress, to garnish			

Bring the stock or water to the boil in the open pressure cooker, add the rice, stir and return to the boil. Adjust the heat so the contents are just boiling but not rising in the cooker. Bring to pressure over the same heat and cook for given time.

Meanwhile, mix the yogurt, lemon juice, oil, herbs, mustard, salt and plenty of freshly ground black pepper together.

Reduce pressure. Strain the rice and return to the open cooker over a low heat, and fluff it up with a fork. Tip into a bowl and fork the dressing and remaining ingredients through the warm rice. Leave to cool completely. Cover then chill.

COOKING TIME High/15-lb pressure 3 minutes
Reduce pressure slowly

SERVES 4–6

54

VEGETABLE CURRY

INGREDIENTS	IMPERIAL	METRIC	AMERICAN
Mustard seeds	3 tsp	3 tsp	3 tsp
Coriander seeds	3 tsp	3 tsp	3 tsp
Cumin seeds	3 tsp	3 tsp	3 tsp
Ghee or oil	3 tbsp	3 tbsp	3 tbsp
Large onion, halved and thinly sliced	1	1	1
Cloves garlic, crushed	2	2	2
Piece fresh root ginger, peeled and thinly sliced	1 inch	2.5 cm	1 inch
Ground turmeric	$1\frac{1}{2}$ tsp	$1\frac{1}{2}$ tsp	$1\frac{1}{2}$ tsp
Chilli powder	$1\frac{1}{2}$ tsp	$1\frac{1}{2}$ tsp	$1\frac{1}{2}$ tsp
Can tomatoes, juice made up to $\frac{1}{2}$ pt/ 300 ml/$1\frac{1}{4}$ cups with vegetable stock or water	14 oz	397 g	1 lb
Tomato purée/paste	2 tsp	2 tsp	2 tsp
Potatoes, cut into large chunks	12 oz	350 g	$\frac{3}{4}$ lb
Carrots, cut into large chunks	8 oz	225 g	$\frac{1}{2}$ lb
Courgettes/zucchini, cut into chunks	8 oz	225 g	$\frac{1}{2}$ lb
Small cauliflower, broken into florets	1	1	1

Block creamed coconut, chopped	$1\frac{1}{2}$ oz	40 g	$1\frac{1}{2}$ oz
Salt and pepper			

Heat the mustard seeds, coriander seeds and cumin seeds together in a small, heavy, non-stick saucepan for 2–3 minutes, shaking the pan occasionally. Crush finely.

Heat the ghee or oil in the open pressure cooker and gently fry the onion and garlic, stirring occasionally, until softened. Add the ginger and continue to cook until the onion is just beginning to colour. Stir in the crushed spices, with the turmeric and chilli powder. Cook gently for 2–3 minutes, then stir in the tomatoes and the tomato juice, tomato purée, potatoes and carrots. Bring to pressure and cook for $1\frac{1}{2}$ minutes. Reduce pressure. Add the courgettes and cauliflower, bring to pressure and cook for given time. Reduce pressure.

Strain off the liquid and reserve. Transfer the vegetables to a warmed serving dish and return the liquid to the cooker. Boil hard in the open cooker until reduced to about 6 fl oz/175 ml/$\frac{3}{4}$ cup. Reduce the heat and stir in the coconut. Continue to stir over a low heat for a few minutes. Adjust the seasoning and flavourings, if necessary. Gently stir in the vegetables and coat them with the sauce.

COOKING TIME High/15-lb pressure first vegetables
   $1\frac{1}{2}$ minutes
   courgettes and cauliflower added $1\frac{1}{2}$ minutes
Reduce pressure quickly

SERVES 4

DHAL

INGREDIENTS	IMPERIAL	METRIC	AMERICAN
Ghee or oil	2 tbsp	2 tbsp	2 tbsp
Onion, cut into rings	1	1	1
Cloves garlic, chopped	3	3	3
Onion seeds	$\frac{1}{2}$ tsp	$\frac{1}{2}$ tsp	$\frac{1}{2}$ tsp
Ground turmeric	$\frac{1}{4}$ tsp	$\frac{1}{4}$ tsp	$\frac{1}{4}$ tsp
Green chilli, sliced	1	1	1
Dried red chilli, slightly slit	1	1	1
Cumin seeds	$\frac{1}{2}$ tsp	$\frac{1}{2}$ tsp	$\frac{1}{2}$ tsp
Red lentils	8 oz	225 g	$\frac{1}{2}$ lb
Vegetable stock	1 pt	550 ml	$2\frac{1}{2}$ cups

Heat the ghee or oil in the open pressure cooker over a medium heat and sauté the onion, stirring occasionally, until browned. Add the garlic. Cook for 1–2 minutes then stir in the onion seeds. Cook until they begin to pop then stir in the turmeric, chilli, cumin and lentils. Stir for 1–2 minutes. Add the stock, bring to the boil in the open cooker over a low heat and skim the scum from the surface. Reduce the heat so the contents are boiling but not rising in the pan. Maintaining the same heat, bring to pressure and cook for given time. Reduce pressure.

Strain the lentils and keep warm. Boil the cooking liquid in the open cooker until almost completely evaporated, then stir back into the lentils.

COOKING TIME Low/5-lb pressure 4 minutes
Reduce pressure slowly

SERVES 4

STUFFED PEPPERS

INGREDIENTS	IMPERIAL	METRIC	AMERICAN
Medium green peppers	4	4	4
Cooked chicken, chopped	8 oz	225 g	$\frac{1}{2}$ lb
Small onions, chopped	2	2	2
Streaky bacon/bacon slices, chopped	4 oz	100 g	$\frac{1}{4}$ lb
Cooked long-grain rice	12 oz	350 g	$\frac{3}{4}$ lb
Ground cumin	1 tsp	1 tsp	1 tsp
Salt and pepper			

Cut off the stem end of the peppers and scoop out the seeds. Mix together the remaining ingredients, seasoning well. Fill each pepper with equal portions of the stuffing mixture. Pour $\frac{1}{2}$ pt/300 ml/$1\frac{1}{4}$ cups water into the pressure cooker and position the trivet. Stand the stuffed peppers on the trivet, bring to pressure and cook for given time. Reduce pressure. Lift the peppers on to a serving dish and garnish them with a few crispy grilled/broiled pieces of bacon, if liked.

COOKING TIME High/15-lb pressure 4 minutes
Reduce pressure quickly

NOTE When reducing pressure, take care not to tilt the pressure cooker, causing the peppers to topple and the stuffing to spill out.

SERVES 4

58

DESSERTS

Fruits, both fresh or dried, custards, milk puddings and sponge puddings are all ideal candidates for pressure-cooking. Enormous time and fuel savings are involved when pressure-cooking most desserts.

Fresh fruits can be quickly cooked or puréed in your pressure cooker and dried fruits need only a few minutes soaking in boiling water before pressure-cooking.

Egg custards cook perfectly without the usual temperature watching. An automatic timer is a 'must' though.

FRUIT HAT

INGREDIENTS	IMPERIAL	METRIC	AMERICAN
Self-raising flour or plain flour sifted with 1 tsp baking powder	4 oz	100 g	1 cup
Pinch salt			
Butter, melted	6 oz	175 g	$\frac{3}{4}$ cup
Fresh white breadcrumbs	4 oz	100 g	2 cups
Large egg, beaten	1	1	1
Milk, to mix			
Stewed or canned fruit such as blackcurrants, plums, cherries	1 lb	450 g	1 lb
Sugar			

Butter a $1\frac{1}{2}$-pt/1-l/4-cup pudding basin.

Sieve together the flour and salt and mix in the melted butter. Stir in the breadcrumbs and mix to a stiff dough with the beaten egg and a little milk. Roll two-thirds of the dough into a circle and use it to line the prepared basin. Put the strained fruit (sweetened to taste) into the pudding and dampen the edges of the dough. Roll the remaining dough into a circle and place it on top of the pudding, sealing the edges before trimming. Cover securely with foil or a double layer of buttered greaseproof/waxed paper.

Pour $1\frac{1}{2}$ pt/1 l/4 cups water into the pressure cooker and position the trivet. Stand the pudding on top. Pre-steam the pudding (see page 70) then bring to pressure and cook for given time. Reduce pressure.

Turn out the pudding. The juice from the strained fruit may be thickened with a little cornflour/cornstarch to make an accompanying sauce.

COOKING TIME Pre-steaming 15 minutes
Low/5-lb pressure 40 minutes
Reduce pressure slowly

SERVES 4

EGG CUSTARD

INGREDIENTS	IMPERIAL	METRIC	AMERICAN
Eggs, beaten	3	3	3
Caster/superfine sugar	2 oz	50 g	$\frac{1}{4}$ cup
Few drops almond essence			
Milk	1 pt	550 ml	$2\frac{1}{2}$ cups
Grated nutmeg			

Mix together the eggs, sugar and almond essence. Warm the milk and blend with the eggs. Pour the mixture into a buttered $1\frac{1}{2}$-pt/1-l/4-cup basin. Sprinkle with a little grated nutmeg and cover securely with foil or a double layer of greaseproof/waxed paper.

Pour 1 pt/550 ml/$2\frac{1}{2}$ cups water into the pressure cooker. Position the trivet and stand the basin on top. Bring to pressure and cook for given time. Reduce pressure.

COOKING TIME High/15-lb pressure 10 minutes
Reduce pressure slowly

NOTE Other flavourings may be used to replace the almond essence. Try vanilla essence or a few teaspoons of instant coffee, dissolved in a little cold water.

SERVES 4

CRÈME BRÛLÉE

INGREDIENTS	IMPERIAL	METRIC	AMERICAN
Single/thin cream	$\frac{1}{2}$ pt	300 ml	$1\frac{1}{4}$ cups
Double/thick cream	$\frac{1}{2}$ pt	300 ml	$1\frac{1}{4}$ cups
Egg yolks	4	4	4
Vanilla essence	1 tsp	1 tsp	1 tsp
Caster/superfine sugar	4–5 tbsp	4–5 tbsp	4–5 tbsp

Butter an ovenproof serving dish. Heat the single and double creams together in a saucepan (but do not allow to boil). Mix together the egg yolks, vanilla essence and 1 tbsp of the sugar, and pour the warmed cream over the eggs. Pour the mixture into the prepared dish and cover it securely with foil.

Pour $\frac{1}{2}$ pt/300 ml/$1\frac{1}{4}$ cups water into the pressure cooker with the trivet. Stand the dish on the trivet. Bring to pressure and cook for given time. Reduce pressure.

Chill the cream for several hours or preferably overnight. Pre-heat the grill/broiler. Dust the top of the cream evenly with the remaining sugar and place it under the grill (at least 4 inches/10 cm away) so the sugar melts and begins to brown. Chill for 2–3 hours before serving. This rich dessert is delicious served with sugared fresh fruit:

COOKING TIME High/15-lb pressure 5 minutes
Reduce pressure slowly

SERVES 4

BREAD AND BUTTER PUDDING

INGREDIENTS	IMPERIAL	METRIC	AMERICAN
Sliced buttered bread, cut into triangles	4–6	4–6	4–6
Sultanas/white raisins	2 oz	50 g	$\frac{1}{3}$ cup
Currants	2 oz	50 g	$\frac{1}{3}$ cup
Caster/superfine sugar	1 oz	25 g	2 tbsp
Milk	$\frac{3}{4}$ pt	400 ml	2 cups
Large eggs, beaten	2	2	2
Grated nutmeg			

Butter a suitable ovenproof dish and layer the bread triangles in the dish with the sultanas, currants and sugar. Warm the milk and pour on to the beaten eggs, stirring well. Pour this mixture over the bread and sprinkle it with grated nutmeg. Cover the basin securely with foil or a double layer of buttered greaseproof/waxed paper. Pour 1 pt/550 ml/2$\frac{1}{2}$ cups water into the pressure cooker. Position the trivet and stand the basin on top. Bring to pressure and cook for given time. Reduce pressure. Brown under a hot grill/broiler to serve.

COOKING TIME High/15-lb pressure 6 minutes
Reduce pressure slowly

SERVES 4

MULLED WINTER FRUIT COMPÔTE

INGREDIENTS	IMPERIAL	METRIC	AMERICAN
Mixed dried fruits, stoned/pitted, e.g. prunes, apricots, pears, peaches, figs	8 oz	225 g	$\frac{1}{2}$ lb
Oranges	2	2	2
Long strip of lemon rind			
Cinnamon stick, halved	1 inch	2.5 cm	1 inch
Cloves	2	2	2
Sweet sherry	$\frac{1}{4}$ pt	150 ml	$\frac{2}{3}$ cup
Sweet white wine	$\frac{1}{4}$ pt	150 ml	$\frac{2}{3}$ cup
Toasted flaked almonds	2 tbsp	2 tbsp	2 tbsp
Whipped cream, fromage blanc or strained Greek yogurt, to serve			

Put the dried fruits into a bowl. Grate the rind and squeeze the juice from 1 of the oranges. Add to the bowl with the lemon rind and spices. Heat the sherry and wine to just below simmering point and pour into the bowl. Cover and leave to soak for 10 minutes.

Pour the contents of the bowl into the pressure cooker. Bring to pressure and cook for 6–8 minutes, depending how soft you like the fruit to be.

Meanwhile, peel the remaining orange and divide into segments. Reduce pressure. Remove the cinnamon stick and serve the compote warm with the orange segments and flaked almonds scattered over. Accompany with whipped cream, fromage blanc or strained Greek yogurt.

COOKING TIME High/15-lb pressure 6–8 minutes
Reduce pressure slowly

SERVES 4

RASPBERRY CREAM

INGREDIENTS	IMPERIAL	METRIC	AMERICAN
Quantity Egg Custard recipe (see page 61)	1	1	1
Can raspberries	1 med	1 med	1 med
Cornflour/cornstarch	1 tbsp	1 tbsp	1 tbsp
Double/thick cream	$\frac{1}{4}$ pt	150 ml	$\frac{2}{3}$ cup
Chopped nuts, to decorate			

Prepare the egg custard, omitting the nutmeg, then cool it slightly. Drain the raspberries and arrange them in a serving bowl. Mix the cornflour with the raspberry juice and bring to the boil, stirring well. Pour this juice over the raspberries and allow it to cool. Stir the cream into the egg custard and pour it over the raspberry mixture. Chill before serving and decorate with chopped nuts.

SERVES 4–6

CHOCOLATE PUDDING

INGREDIENTS	IMPERIAL	METRIC	AMERICAN
Margarine	4 oz	100 g	$\frac{1}{2}$ cup
Caster/superfine sugar	4 oz	100 g	$\frac{1}{2}$ cup
Large eggs, beaten	2	2	2
Self-raising flour or plain flour sifted with $1\frac{1}{2}$ tsp baking powder	6 oz	150 g	$1\frac{1}{2}$ cups
Cocoa powder	2 tsp	2 tsp	2 tsp
Chopped plain/ semi-sweet chocolate	4 oz	100 g	$\frac{1}{2}$ cup
Milk, to mix			

Butter a 1-pt/550-ml/2$\frac{1}{2}$-cup pudding basin. Cream the margarine and sugar until light and fluffy, and gradually beat in the egg. Sieve together the flour and cocoa powder and fold them gently into the mixture along with the chopped chocolate. Add a little milk if necessary to make a smooth dropping consistency. Put the mixture into the prepared basin and cover it securely with foil or a double layer of buttered greaseproof/waxed paper.

Pour $1\frac{1}{2}$ pt/1 l/4 cups water into the pressure cooker. Position the trivet and stand the pudding on top. Pre-steam the pudding (see page 70) then bring to pressure and cook for given time. Reduce pressure. Serve with custard or sweet white sauce.

COOKING TIME Pre-steaming 25 minutes
Low/5-lb pressure 25 minutes
Reduce pressure slowly

SERVES 4

VANILLA RICE PUDDING

INGREDIENTS	IMPERIAL	METRIC	AMERICAN
Butter	1 oz	25 g	2 tbsp
Milk	1 pt	550 ml	$2\frac{1}{2}$ cups
Pudding rice	2 oz	50 g	$\frac{1}{3}$ cup
Sugar	2 oz	50 g	$\frac{1}{4}$ cup
Vanilla essence	1 tsp	1 tsp	1 tsp
Good pinch grated nutmeg			

Melt the butter in the open pressure cooker without the trivet and pour in the milk. Bring to the boil and add the remaining ingredients. Bring to the boil again, then lower the heat so that the milk simmers gently. Bring to pressure on this heat and cook for given time. Reduce pressure.

Stir the pudding and pour it into a warmed serving dish. If liked, brown it under a hot grill/broiler before serving.

COOKING TIME High/15-lb pressure 12 minutes
Reduce pressure slowly

NOTE Try using cinnamon or mixed spice to replace the vanilla and nutmeg.

SERVES 4

CHRISTMAS PUDDING

INGREDIENTS	IMPERIAL	METRIC	AMERICAN
Self-raising flour or plain flour sifted with $\frac{1}{2}$-tsp baking powder	2 oz	50 g	$\frac{1}{2}$ cup
Pinch salt			
Each of, grated nutmeg, mixed spice, cinnamon	$\frac{1}{2}$ tsp	$\frac{1}{2}$ tsp	$\frac{1}{2}$ tsp
Fresh white breadcrumbs	3 oz	75 g	$1\frac{1}{2}$ cups
Beef suet, shredded or finely chopped	3 oz	75 g	$\frac{2}{3}$ cup
Demerara/brown sugar	2 oz	50 g	$\frac{1}{4}$ cup
Each, currants, raisins, sultanas/white raisins, mixed peel	4 oz	100 g	$\frac{2}{3}$ cup
Chopped almonds	1 oz	25 g	$\frac{1}{4}$ cup
Eggs, beaten	2	2	2
Grated rind and juice of 1 orange			
Brandy	2 tbsp	2 tbsp	2 tbsp
Milk, ale or stout, to mix			

Butter two 1-pt/550 ml/$2\frac{1}{2}$-cup pudding basins. Sieve the flour with the salt and spices. Add all dry ingredients and mix well. Mix together the beaten eggs, orange rind and juice, brandy and a little milk. Add these to the fruit mixture and stir well. Turn into the prepared basins and cover securely with foil or a double layer of buttered greaseproof/waxed paper. Pour $2\frac{1}{2}$ pt/1.5 l/$6\frac{1}{4}$ cups water into the pressure cooker and position the trivet. Stand the puddings on the trivet. Pre-steam the puddings for the time shown then bring to pressure and cook for given time. Reduce pressure. Serve with brandy sauce.

COOKING TIME Pre-steaming 20 minutes
High/15-lb pressure $1\frac{3}{4}$ hours
Reduce pressure slowly

REHEATING TIME High/15-lb pressure 20 minutes
Reduce pressure slowly

CHECKPOINT The puddings should be prepared in October so that they have time to mature before Christmas. If your pressure cooker is large enough, cook the puddings side by side on the trivet, or one on top of the other with the trivet between. The basins must not touch the sides or the lid.

MAKES 2 × 1 lb/450 g puddings

APRICOT CONDÉ

INGREDIENTS	IMPERIAL	METRIC	AMERICAN
Quantity Vanilla Rice Pudding (see page 67)	1	1	1
Single/thin cream	2 tbsp	2 tbsp	2 tbsp
Cooked dried apricots			

Cook the rice pudding as indicated in the recipe and allow it to cool. Mix the cold rice pudding with a little cream and some drained chopped apricots. Spoon it into individual dishes and decorate with more fruit.

NOTE This may be served with cooked fresh or canned fruit.

SERVES 4

STEAMED PUDDINGS

An ovenproof container should be used for puddings. The container should not be more than two-thirds full — the pudding must have space to rise. When covering the pudding make a pleat in the foil or greaseproof/waxed paper in case the pudding rises above the rim and secure the foil or greaseproof paper firmly on to the container, preferably with string.

Refer to your manufacturers' instructions about the amount of water needed, it will depend on the cooking time but should not be less than 1½ pt/1 1/4 cups.

Water should not boil while preparing the pudding or you may not have sufficient water left for cooking. Put boiling water into the pressure cooker rather than bring cold water to the boil.

The trivet is used as a stand for the pudding.

Puddings are usually pre-steamed before pressure cooking to produce a light texture in the finished pudding. At the end of the pre-steaming period, the pressure weight or rotating valve is placed in position and the pressure cooker is brought to pressure for the required time.

Pressure should be reduced slowly.

When converting your own recipes for pressure-cooking the following guide may be useful:

Normal steaming time	Pre-steaming time	Pressure-cooking time
		Low/5-lb
30 minutes	5 minutes	10 minutes
1 hour	15 minutes	25 minutes
2–3 hours	20 minutes	50–60 minutes

PRESERVES AND BOTTLING

If you are lover of home-made preserves and bottled fruit, your pressure cooker will be a great time-saver.

Fruit for marmalades, jams and jellies is softened under pressure. When the sugar is added, the pressure cooker is used like an ordinary saucepan, without the lid, until the preserve reaches setting point.

Chutney ingredients are cooked under pressure, then reduced and thickened in the open pressure cooker for potting.

Bottling fruit is a simple and attractive way of preserving fresh, ripe summer produce.

APPLE CHUTNEY

INGREDIENTS	IMPERIAL	METRIC	AMERICAN
Cooking apples, peeled, cored and diced	2 lb	1 kg	2 lb
Onions, chopped	2 lb	1 kg	2 lb
Sultanas/white raisins	4 oz	100 g	$\frac{2}{3}$ cup
Malt vinegar	$\frac{1}{2}$ pt	300 ml	$1\frac{1}{4}$ cups
Grated rind and juice of 1 lemon			
Ground cloves	1 tsp	1 tsp	1 tsp
Ground cinnamon	1 tsp	1 tsp	1 tsp
Ground ginger	1 tsp	1 tsp	1 tsp
Salt	1 tsp	1 tsp	1 tsp
Demerara/brown sugar	12 oz	350 g	$\frac{3}{4}$ lb

Place the apples, onions and sultanas in the pressure cooker with the vinegar, without the trivet. Bring to pressure and cook for given time. Reduce pressure. Add the remaining ingredients and heat them gently until the sugar dissolves. Bring to the boil and simmer in the open pressure cooker until the chutney thickens. Pour into warmed, dry jars. Cover and label.

COOKING TIME High/15-lb pressure 12 minutes
Reduce pressure slowly

MAKES ABOUT 4 lb/1.8 kg

LEMON CURD

INGREDIENTS	IMPERIAL	METRIC	AMERICAN
Eggs, beaten	4	4	4
Sugar	1 lb	450 g	1 lb
Finely grated rind of 4 lemons			
Lemons, strained juice	2	2	2
Unsalted butter, cut into small pieces	4 oz	100 g	$\frac{1}{2}$ cup

Strain the beaten eggs into an ovenproof basin and stir in the sugar, lemon rind, lemon juice and butter pieces. Securely tie on a double layer of buttered greaseproof/waxed paper. Pour $\frac{1}{2}$ pt/300 ml/$1\frac{1}{4}$ cups water into the pressure cooker and position the trivet. Stand the basin on the trivet, bring to pressure and cook for given time. Reduce pressure. Stir the lemon curd and pour into warmed, dry jars. Cool, cover and label.

COOKING TIME High/15-lb pressure 10 minutes
Reduce pressure slowly

NOTE Lemon Curd may be stored for up to 2 months only.

MAKES ABOUT 2 lb/1 kg

ORANGE MARMALADE

INGREDIENTS	IMPERIAL	METRIC	AMERICAN
Seville oranges	$1\frac{1}{2}$ lb	700 g	$1\frac{1}{2}$ lb
Water	1 pt	550 ml	$2\frac{1}{2}$ cups
Juice 1 lemon			
Sugar	3 lb	1.4 kg	3 lb

Remove the peel from the oranges, using a sharp knife or potato peeler and making sure no pith is attached. Cut the peel into pieces. Cut the oranges in half and squeeze out the juice. Tie the pith and pips in a piece of muslin/cheesecloth and soak in the water overnight. Place the water, muslin bag, peel and lemon juice in the pressure cooker. Bring to pressure and cook for given time. Reduce pressure.

Cool the liquid sufficiently to squeeze the juice from the muslin bag into the orange liquor. Stir in the sugar. Discard the muslin bag. Heat the marmalade gently until the sugar dissolves, then boil it rapidly in the open pressure cooker until setting point is reached (see page 75). To prevent the peel rising in the jars, cool the marmalade until a skin begins to form on top (about 15 minutes), then pour it into warmed, dry jars and cover with wax discs. Cool, cover and label.

COOKING TIME High/15-lb pressure 10–15 minutes
Reduce pressure slowly

MAKES 4–5 lb/1.8–2.3 kg

MARMALADES, JAMS AND JELLIES

When softening fruit under pressure, fill the pressure cooker no more than half full.

The trivet is not used.

Choose fresh, ripe, firm, unblemished fruit for a good result.

Softening the fruit helps to release the pectin (the setting agent) in fruit. Some fruits contain more than others, and you may need to mix fruits or to add lemon to compensate.

High-pectin fruits: damsons, blackcurrants, redcurrants, gooseberries.

Medium-pectin fruits: apricots, greengages, loganberries, plums, raspberries.

Low-pectin fruits: blackberries, cherries, marrow, pears, rhubarb, strawberries.

Warmed sugar will take less time to dissolve and will produce a preserve of better colour and flavour.

Once the sugar has been added the lid *must not* be replaced on the pressure cooker. Use the pressure cooker base as an ordinary pan.

There are three methods of checking that the jam has reached setting point:

1. The temperature test is the most accurate method. The jam will set when it reaches a temperature of 221°F (104°C).

2. Place a little of the jam on to a cold plate. When the jam is cool, push your finger across its surface. If it wrinkles, you must have a set. During this test remember to move the pressure cooker off the heat to avoid boiling the jam too long.

3. Stir the jam with a wooden spoon and lift it out. The

jam will begin to set on the spoon when setting point is reached.

When adapting your own recipes for pressure-cooking, reduce the liquid by about half (but make sure you include the minimum amount recommended in your instruction book). Generally, allow 1 lb/450 g sugar per 1 lb/450 g fruit.

ALMOND APRICOT JAM

INGREDIENTS	IMPERIAL	METRIC	AMERICAN
Dried apricots, washed and cup up	1 lb	450 g	1 lb
Boiling water	2 pt	1 l	5 cups
Juice 1 lemon			
Sugar	3 lb	1.4 kg	3 lb
Blanched almonds	2 oz	50 g	$\frac{1}{3}$ cup

Put the apricots in the pressure cooker with the boiling water, without the trivet. Cover and leave for 1 hour. Add the lemon juice, bring to pressure and cook for given time. Reduce pressure.

Add the sugar and heat gently until it dissolves. Stir in the almonds and boil the jam rapidly in the open pressure cooker until setting point is reached (see page 75). Pour the jam into warmed, dry jars and cover with waxed discs. Cool, cover and label.

COOKING TIME High/15-lb pressure 10 minutes
Reduce pressure slowly

MAKES 4–5 lb/1.8–2.3 kg

DAMSON AND PORT JAM

INGREDIENTS	IMPERIAL	METRIC	AMERICAN
Damsons	3 lb	1.4 kg	3 lb
Water	$\frac{1}{2}$ pt	300 ml	$1\frac{1}{4}$ cups
Preserving sugar, warmed	3 lb	1.4 kg	3 lb
Port	4 tbsp	4 tbsp	4 tbsp
Knob of butter			

Wash and dry the fruit and prick each damson 2–3 times with a knitting needle. Put the fruit and water into the pressure cooker. Bring to pressure and cook for given time. Reduce pressure.

Add the sugar to the open cooker and stir over a low heat until the sugar has completely dissolved. Boil rapidly until setting point is reached, about 20 minutes. Remove from the heat and stir in the port and a small knob of butter. Remove the stones using a slotted spoon. Pour the jam into warmed, dry jars. Cover and label.

COOKING TIME Medium/10-lb pressure 8 minutes
Reduce pressure slowly

MAKES ABOUT 5 lb/2.3 kg

APPLE JELLY

INGREDIENTS	IMPERIAL	METRIC	AMERICAN
Cooking apples	3 lb	1.4 kg	3 lb
Juice 1 lemon			
Water	1 pt	550 ml	$2\frac{1}{2}$ cups

Proportion of sugar to strained juice 1 lb/450 g per	1 pt	550 ml	$2\frac{1}{2}$ cups

Wash the apples, removing any bruised parts, and cut them into thick slices (but do not peel or core them). Place the apples in the pressure cooker with the lemon juice and water, without the trivet. Bring to pressure and cook for given time. Reduce pressure.

Mash the apples and strain them through a jelly bag or double layer of cloth (such as a tea towel or sheeting). Measure the strained juice and put it back into the pressure cooker with the correct amount of sugar. Heat gently until the sugar dissolves, then boil rapidly in the open pressure cooker until setting point is reached (see page 75). Pour the jelly into warmed, dry jars and cover with wax discs. Cool, cover and label.

COOKING TIME High/15-lb pressure 3 minutes
Reduce pressure slowly

CHECKPOINT If the juice is allowed to drip through the jelly bag or cloth, the result will be clearer than if it is forced through.

REDCURRANT JELLY

As for apple jelly, using 3 lb/1.4 kg redcurrants with $\frac{1}{2}$ pt/300 ml/$1\frac{1}{4}$ cups water. To each 1 pt/550 ml/$2\frac{1}{2}$ cups strained juice add $1\frac{1}{4}$ lb/550 g sugar.

BLACKCURRANT JELLY

As for apple jelly, using 3 lb/1.4 kg blackcurrants with $1\frac{3}{4}$ pt/1 l/$4\frac{1}{2}$ cups water. To each 1 pt/550 ml/$2\frac{1}{2}$ cups strained juice add 1 lb/450 g sugar.

BOTTLING

CHECKPOINTS FOR BOTTLING FRUIT The trivet should be used for bottling.

Remember to add to the pressure cooker at least the minimum amount of water recommended by your manufacturer. Check the instruction book for your particular pressure cooker.

Choose bottles which will fit easily into the pressure cooker. When stood on the trivet, they should not touch each other or the sides or lid of the pressure cooker.

Make sure the bottling jars are not damaged in any way. The rubber rings must be flexible and fit the neck of the jar snugly.

Fruits should be ripe, firm and unblemished. Choose fruits of similar size and ripeness.

Fruit can be bottled in water, but a better result is obtained if a syrup is used. To make syrup:

Light syrup: suitable for fruit to be used for tarts, crumbles etc. Boil 2–4 oz/50–100 g/4–8 tbsp sugar in each 1 pt/550 ml/$2\frac{1}{2}$ cups water.

Heavy syrup: suitable for fruit to be used straight as a dessert or for soft fruits which are liable to float in the jar. Boil 6–8 oz/175–225 g/$\frac{3}{4}$–1 cup sugar in each 1 pt/550 ml/$2\frac{1}{2}$ cups water.

TO BOTTLE FRUIT Wash and rinse the jars and lids. Stand them in boiling water till ready to use.

Wash the fruit and prepare according to kind. Pack it firmly into the jars to the shoulder.

Pour boiling syrup over the fruit, leaving $\frac{1}{4}$ inch/0.5 cm headspace. To eliminate air bubbles, pour in a little syrup at a time, tapping the jar gently after each addition.

Fit rubber band and tops on the jars. With metal screw bands, screw on till tight, then unscrew turn. Jars with metal clips should be sealed.

Place the trivet in the pressure cooker with boiling water (check with instruction book for correct amount, usually about 2 pt/1.1 l/5 cups. Stand the jars on the trivet.

Bring to pressure on medium heat and cook for given time (see chart following). Reduce pressure slowly.

Fruit	Cooking time at Medium/10-lb pressure
Apples, quarters, thick slices	1 minute
Apricots, whole	1 minute
Blackberries	1 minute
Blackcurrants, Redcurrants	1 minute
Cherries, whole	1 minute
Damsons, Greengages, Plums, whole	1 minute
Gooseberries	1 minute
Peaches, skinned halves	3 minutes
Pears, peeled, cored and halved	3 minutes
Raspberries	1 minute
Rhubarb	1 minute
Strawberries	3 minutes
Tomatoes, skinned, whole	3 minutes

PRESSURE COOKING TIME CHARTS

MEAT
The following times for pressure-cooking joints are for High/15-lb pressure.

	Cooking time per lb/450 g at High/ 15-lb pressure
Beef	
Rolled sirloin or rump	10 minutes
Topside, rolled rump	12 minutes
Silverside	15 minutes
Lamb	
Breast, boned and rolled	12 minutes
Leg	15 minutes
Pork	
Fillet	12 minutes
Shoulder or loin, boned and rolled	15 minutes
Veal	
Knuckle	10 minutes
Fillet, loin	12 minutes
Shoulder, boned or breast, boned and rolled	14 minutes
Bacon	12 minutes
Ox tongue	15 minutes

POULTRY AND GAME
The following times for pressure-cooking poultry and game are for High/15-lb pressure.

Poultry and Game		Cooking time at High/15-lb pressure
Chicken:		
Poussin,	halved	7 minutes
	joints	4 minutes
Roasting,	whole	5 minutes per 1 lb/450 g
	joints	5–7 minutes (depending on size)
Boiling,	whole	10 minutes per 1 lb/450 g
	joints	10–15 minutes (depending on size)
Turkey,	joints	10 minutes
Duck,	whole	12–15 minutes per 1 lb/450 g
	joints	12 minutes
Grouse		10 minutes
Pigeons		10 minutes
Hare,	joints	40 minutes
Rabbit,	joints	15 minutes
Pheasant,	whole	7–10 minutes (depending on age)
Partridge		
	joints	5–7 minutes (depending on age)

FISH
The following times for pressure-cooking fish are for High/15-lb pressure.

White fish	Cooking time at High/15-lb pressure
Bass, Bream, Brill,	Steaks and fillets 3–6 minutes

82

Cod, Coley, Haddock, Hake, Halibut, Ling, Plaice, Rock Salmon, Sole, Turbot	Whole fish 5–6 minutes per 1 lb/450 g
Skate wings	3–6 minutes
Whiting	Steaks and fillets 4–5 minutes Whole fish 5–6 minutes per 1 lb/450 g

Oily fish	
Herring, Mackerel, Mullet, Trout	Whole fish 5–8 minutes
Salmon	Steaks 6–8 minutes Whole fish 6 minutes per 1 lb/450 g

Shellfish	
Crab	7–10 minutes
Lobster	10 minutes
Prawns, Shrimps	2–3minutes

VEGETABLES

The following times for pressure-cooking fresh vegetables are for High/15-lb pressure. Blanching times are for Medium/10-lb pressure only.

Vegetable	*Cooking time High/15-lb pressure*	*Blanching time Medium/10-lb pressure*
Artichokes, Globe	6–10 minutes depending on size	3–5 minutes depending on size
Jerusalem	4–6 minutes	
Asparagus, bundles	2–4 minutes	bring to pressure only
Beans, Broad	3–5 minutes	1 minute
French	3 minutes	bring to pressure only

Runner	4 minutes	bring to pressure only
Beetroot/Beet, small	10 minutes	7 minutes, sliced
medium	15–20 minutes	
large	20–30 minutes	
Broccoli spears	3–4 minutes	1 minute
Brussels Sprouts	3–4 minutes	1 minute
Cabbage, shredded	3 minutes	bring to pressure only
Carrots, sliced	3–4 minutes	2 minutes
Cauliflower, florets	3–4 minutes	1 minute
whole	5–8 minutes	
Celery, short sticks	3 minutes	2 minutes
Celeriac, cubes	3 minutes	1 minute
Chicory, whole	3–6 minutes	
Corn on the cob	3–5 minutes depending on size	2–3 minutes depending on size
Courgettes/zucchini, sliced	3 minutes	bring to pressure only
Fennel, halves	3–6 minutes	1 minute
Leeks, sliced	3–4 minutes	1 minute
Marrow, thick slices	3–4 minutes	2 minutes
Onions, whole	6–8 minutes	
sliced	3–4 minutes	
Parsnips, sliced	3–4 minutes	1 minute
Peas	3–4 minutes	1 minute
Potatoes, new whole	4–5 minutes	2 minutes
old quarters	3–4 minutes	
Spinach	1–2 minutes	bring to pressure only
Swede, cubes	4 minutes	1 minute
Turnip, sliced or small whole	3–4 minutes	2 minutes

DRIED VEGETABLES

Dried vegetables do not need overnight soaking. Put the vegetables into a large bowl and cover them with plenty of boiling water. Put a plate over the bowl and leave the beans to soak for one hour.

Pour into the pressure cooker $1\frac{3}{4}$ pt/1 l/4$\frac{1}{2}$ cups liquid for every 1 lb/450 g vegetables. Make up the soaking water from the vegetables to the required amount with more water.

Bring to the boil and add the vegetables. The pressure cooker should not be more than half full. Season to taste and bring it back to the boil.

Skim the surface of the liquid, then lower the heat till the contents boil gently. Bring to pressure on this heat and cook for the given time.

Always reduce pressure slowly.

Dried vegetable	Cooking time at High/15-lb pressure
Butter/lima beans	20 minutes
Haricot/navy beans, small	20 minutes
large	30 minutes
Lentils	15 minutes
Peas, whole	20 minutes
split	15 minutes

NOTE Split varieties, such as lentils or peas, may be added to soups, casseroles etc., without pre-soaking.

FRESH FRUIT

Fruit	Cooking time at High/15-lb pressure
Apricots, Cherries, Damsons,	Bring to pressure

Greengages (halved)	
Pears, Peaches (halved)	3–5 minutes
Hard pears	8–10 minutes
	Medium/10-lb pressure
Blackcurrants,	Bring to
Gooseberries,	pressure
Loganberries,	only on
Raspberries,	medium
Plums, Rhubarb	heat
Apple (slices)	1 minute

DRIED FRUIT

Place the fruit in a bowl and cover it with boiling water. Pour over 1 pt/550 ml/2½ cups for every 1 lb/450 g dried fruit. Cover with a plate and leave to stand for 10 minutes.

Place the fruit and soaking liquid in the pressure cooker (without the trivet) and add sugar and flavourings (such as lemon or orange rind and juice, cloves, spices) to taste.

Do not fill the pressure cooker more than half full, as the fruit will expand during cooking.

Bring to pressure and cook for given time (see table below). Reduce pressure slowly.

Fruit	*Cooking time at High/15-lb pressure*
Apples	6 minutes
Apricots	3 minutes
Figs, Pears, Prunes, Mixed Fruit	10 minutes
Peaches	5 minutes

HOW TO USE YOUR PRESSURE COOKER

It is essential to follow the manufacturers' instructions for your particular model very carefully to obtain good results. When giving general instructions for use below, I have separated the main sorts of pressure cookers into types.

Type 1 has a Speedset pressure control.

Type 2 has a pressure weight with an indicator plunger (Weight A, diagram p. 88).

Type 3 has a pressure weight consisting of fitted rings (Weight B, diagram p. 88).

Type 4 has a fixed 7½-lb pressure (diagram p. 88).

TYPES 1, 2 AND 3

1. Put the prepared food into the pressure cooker along with the accurate amount of liquid. Usually the minimum amount needed is ½ pt/300 ml/1¼ cups, but check the manufacturers' instructions to make sure. The quantity required will depend on the recipe being followed and the length of cooking time. The liquid used must always be one which gives off steam when it boils, e.g. water, stock, fruit juice, cider, wine.

Remember to leave sufficient space above the food for steam to circulate or for foods to rise in the pressure cooker.

2. Place the lid in position, ensuring that it is firmly locked.

3. Place the pressure cooker on the heat.

Type 2

Type 3

(A) Indicator Weight

(B) Pressure Weights

Sealing Gasket

Sealing Gasket

Trivet

Trivet

Separators

Separator

Type 4

Rotating valve

Lid with Clamp

Sealing Gasket

Divider

Raised Basket

TYPE 1

4. Clip the Speedset pressure control on to the steam vent. The lever must be switched so it is pointing to the '0' on the housing.

5. As the temperature inside the cooker increases the air will be expelled and the automatic air vent (under the housing) will seal.

6. Once the pressure begins to increase the visual indicator inside the Speedset pressure control will begin to rise. The indicator consists of three coloured bands to correspond with the pressure given in the recipes:

Yellow band	Low/5-lb pressure
Blue band	Medium/10-lb pressure
Red band	High/15-lb pressure

Once the desired colour band is *just* showing the pressure required, reduce the heat to maintain this pressure.

TYPE 2

4. Place the indicator weight firmly in position on the central vent and turn the heat up full.

5. As the liquid boils, the pressure cooker fills with steam, some of which will be seen coming through the automatic air vent. This air vent will seal itself automatically, then the indicator plunger will rise as the pressure rises.

6. When the required pressure has been reached, shown by the number of silver rings (or coloured bands as on Type 1), turn the heat down to maintain this pressure.
   Time the cooking from now.

TYPE 3

4. Place the correct weight firmly in position on the central vent. Turn the heat up full.

5. As the liquid boils, the pressure cooker fills with steam, expelling all the air. When the pressure builds up

sufficiently inside the pressure cooker a slight hissing sound will be heard, followed by a much louder one as steam begins to escape. Do not leave the pressure cooker during this stage.

6. A continuous loud hissing indicates that pressure has now been reached, so turn down the heat until a continuous gentle 'muttering' is heard. This should be maintained throughout the cooking time.

Time the cooking from now.

TYPES 1, 2 AND 3

7. At the end of the cooking time, remove the pressure cooker from the heat. Pressure must be reduced before removing the pressure weight or the lid. There are two methods of doing this.

a. *Slow method*

This slower method should be used when:

cooking liquid foods (such as soups and stews) and dried vegetables, all of which are liable to spurt out of the vent pipe on sudden reduction of pressure.

cooking egg custards and milk puddings which would curdle or separate with a sudden temperature drop, cooking puddings containing a raising agent, which would sink with a sudden temperature drop, and bottling, where a sudden temperature drop would cause the jars to crack.

TYPES 1 AND 2

Reduce pressure slowly by allowing the pressure cooker to stand at room temperature, away from the heat, until the indicator plunger has dropped so no silver rings or coloured bands are visible, and the metal plunger if there is one in the automatic air vent has dropped to its normal position. The weight if there is one can now be lifted off and the lid removed.

TYPE 3
Reduce pressure slowly by allowing the pressure cooker to stand at room temperature, away from the heat. To test whether pressure has been reduced, lift the weight slightly. When no more steam escapes the weight can be lifted off and the lid removed.

b. *Quick method*
TYPE 1
Reduce pressure quickly by turning the pressure release lever to the left to the 'steam' position. Steam and pressure will be released through the steam housing.

TYPES 2 AND 3
Reduce pressure with cold water by standing the pressure cooker in a bowl of cold water.

This method should be used when the cooking time is vital. For example, vegetables would overcook if pressure was not reduced this way.

NOTE Each recipe in this book indicates the correct method for reducing pressure.

TYPE 4
1. Put the prepared food into the pressure cooker with the correct amount of liquid (refer to the manufacturers' instructions on the minimum quantity needed for particular recipes or methods of cooking). Remember that the liquid used must be one which gives off steam when it boils and do leave sufficient space above the food for steam to circulate or for foods to rise.
2. Place the lid in position by sliding it on horizontally and fitting it carefully on to the rim of the pan. To tighten the lid, turn the knob in the direction of the arrow through two complete turns. The lid is now tight and locked.
3. Position the rotating valve by placing it vertically on the vent on the lid and push down as far as it will go.

4. Place the pressure cooker on the heat. As pressure is reached the valve begins to turn, emitting steam. *Time cooking from now.* Reduce the heat so that the valve remains still most of the time. A little steam will still be released, and the valve will occasionally turn slowly.

5. At the end of the cooking time, remove the pressure cooker from the heat. Lower the pressure by lifting the rotating valve up to the first notch (do not remove it completely). This allows the steam to escape while the pressure falls. When all the steam has been expelled the lid can be removed. Do this by turning the knob in the opposite direction to the arrow until the clamp touches the lid. Lift the lid and slide it out horizontally.

If pressure is not reduced as soon as cooking is completed, the cooling steam condenses inside the pressure cooker, forming a vacuum and thus holding down the lid. If this should happen, reheat the pressure cooker for a few seconds with the knob in the open position. The lid will loosen itself.

NOTE Since more steam is lost during cooking with pressure cooker Type 4, more liquid is needed. Cooking times will be longer than those for Types 1, 2 and 3 as the cooking pressure is lower.

SAFETY

All pressure cookers include safety devices which operate if the vent pipe becomes blocked or if the pressure cooker boils dry and over-heats. Should the safety devices come into operation, the excess pressure is automatically released from the pressure cooker. However, if the manufacturers' instructions are carefully followed, the safety devices should never need to activate.

As a general rule, never fill the pressure cooker more than two-thirds full with solids or half-full with liquids or other foods that tend to boil over (for example, soups, milk, cereals, pastas). Sufficient space must always be left above the food for steam to circulate and for foods to rise.

WEIGHTS AND MEASURES

Ingredients used in the recipes are given in Imperial, Metric and American measures. Generally speaking, the metric and American measures are not exact equivalents of their imperial counterparts. I find it better to work in quantities which have been rounded off to convenient measures. Where I have felt it important to be accurate, exact equivalents are given. It is wise to follow one set of measures throughout a recipe; do not skip from one set to another.

All spoon and cup measures are level unless otherwise stated.

The imperial pint measures 20 fl oz; the American pint measures 16 fl oz.

When cans of food are included in a recipe, the weights given on the label are quoted – these are usually exact equivalents.

When converting your own recipes from imperial to metric quantities, or vice versa, use the following tables as guidelines.

CAPACITY

Imperial	Metric
$\frac{1}{4}$ pt (5 fl oz)	150 ml
$\frac{1}{2}$ pt (10 fl oz)	300 ml
$\frac{3}{4}$ pt (15 fl oz)	400 ml
1 pt (20 fl oz)	500–600 ml
$1\frac{1}{2}$ pt	900 ml
$1\frac{3}{4}$ pt	1 l
2 pt	1.1 l

WEIGHT

Imperial	Metric
1 oz	25 g
2 oz	50 g
3 oz	75 g
4 oz	100–125 g
5 oz	150 g
6 oz	175 g
8 oz	225 g
10 oz	275 g
12 oz	350 g
14 oz	400 g
16 oz (1 lb)	450 g
1½ lb	700 g
2 lb	900 g
3 lb	1.4 kg

QUANTITIES

Most of the recipes in this book are for four people. Some are for six or occasionally more.

These quantities may be halved or quartered as long as the minimum amount of liquid recommended in your instruction book is included. Remember that the amount of liquid used depends on the cooking time and on the size of your pressure cooker, and *not* on the amount of food being cooked.

When doubling up on quantities, check the appropriate section of the book to see how full the pressure cooker should be.

INDEX